# felt me a Smile

for you

toyoko sugiwaka

POTTER
CRAFT

# Smile more

# To make something for someone.

Make something for someone with a feeling
of warmheartedness — this will surely make you smile.
That smile can hopefully be passed on to your "someone."

## Smiles are coming.
If you smile, your mind opens automatically.
If your mind is open, you will appreciate every little,
good thing. Take care: the little things are easy to overlook
in daily life.

# contents

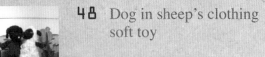
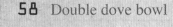

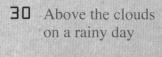

GOOD HEART
QUALITY

**First step**
Take a look at these
little wonders —
just relax and enjoy.

felt me a Smile

# GALLERY

dog in sheep's clothing soft toy

# LEAD ME
# TO BELIEVE

A Brief, Blissful Moment

come to me

HAPPINESS IS ATTAINED BY INNER PEACE

wiener dog draft stopper

disinterestedness mother

meditation rabbits meeting at 3am

INTROVERT
CAT WITH
GUTS

introvert cat with guts

gentle owl necklace holder

HER SMILE IS SMALL

twinkle
twinkle
little
toes

*I have tiny wings, but I can fly into the big sky*

donkeys on holiday

above the clouds on a rainy day

A hip cat has
experiential knowledge

I am always by your side

world's happiest posture

# SMILE MORE
# DEAR

# Good heart quality

When you feel happy, and
you wish to be useful to others,
then you can make good,
heartfelt things.
Make things with heart, stitch by stitch, with
gentle and calm feelings, and your work will
be very special.

# Favorite things,
# no reason necessary

Imagine ten of your favorite things.
Things that are not absolutely necessary but which
are nice to have around you. Favorite things that
you have collected one by one.
They will be your source of creativity.

# Imagination is creation

While you are thinking about creating something,
you may make happy discoveries by accident.
When you really concentrate and
use your imagination, you become
like a magnet: things and people
are drawn to you.

# felt me a Smile
# WORKSHOP

### Second step
Got the idea?
Now, learn how to make
these things.
You can arrange and make
your own smiley stuff!

# Dog in sheep's clothing soft toy

Make the black dog and his white wool coat. The black dog uses his coat when he would like to understand the sheep's mind.

## Materials
(Black dog)
Fine yarn in black, red, and light blue; bead (for nose); toy stuffing
(Sheep coat)
White wool roving; raw fleece kid curls

## Tools
Size C crochet hook; wool sewing needle; soap; bubble wrap

### WELCOME TO THE SINGLE-CROCHET WORLD

Wrap yarn twice around two fingers and hold the doubled yarn in one hand. Wrap yarn around hook and bring it to the front.

Wrap the yarn over the hook. Draw the yarn through the loop.

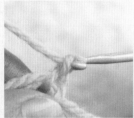   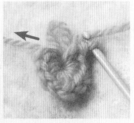

**CHAIN STITCH**
Wrap the yarn over the crochet hook and draw the yarn through the loop on the hook to make one chain (1ch).

**SINGLE CROCHET**
Insert the hook into the doubled yarn, wrap the yarn over the hook, then draw the yarn through.

Wrap the yarn over the hook and draw it through two loops. Make 10 single crochet (10sc) in the loop.

Pull yarn tail until one loop begins to tighten, then pull the tight loop to adjust the other loop, then pull the tail until both loops are tight.

**SLIP STITCH**
Insert the hook into the first stitch of the round and wrap the yarn over the hook.

Draw the yarn through both the stitch and the loop on the hook to make a slip stitch (ss).

**FINISH A ROUND**
Make 1ch to begin each round. Work sc into stitches of the previous round until desired length is attained.

After the ss in the last round, cut the yarn tail and draw the tail of yarn through the loop. Pull the yarn firmly.

## LEGS

| | |
|---|---|
| **Round 1** | 1ch, 10sc in double ring, tighten and ss to make circle. |
| **Round 2** | 1ch, 12sc (work 2sc in the same stitches every fifth stitch of previous round). |
| **Round 3** | 1ch, 14sc (work 2sc in every sixth stitch). |
| **Round 4** | 1ch, 17sc (work 2sc in every fourth stitch). |
| **Round 5** | 1ch, 21sc (work 2sc in every fourth stitch). |
| **Rounds 6–22** | 1ch, 21sc. |

## ARMS

Work as for legs until Round 3.
**Rounds 4–16** 1ch, 14sc.

## NOSE & EAR

Work as for legs until Round 4.
**Rounds 5–13** 1ch, 17sc.
Leave a yarn tail 16 in. long.

**SC** SINGLE CROCHET

**ch** CHAIN STITCH

**ss** SLIP STITCH

## HEAD

| | |
|---|---|
| **Round 1** | 1ch, 10sc in double ring, tighten and ss to make circle. |
| **Round 2** | 1ch, 15sc (work 2sc in same stitch every second stitch of previous round). |
| **Round 3** | 1ch, 18sc (work 2sc in every fifth stitch). |
| **Round 4** | 1ch, 22sc (work 2sc in every fourth stitch). |
| **Round 5** | 1ch, 27sc (work 2sc in every fourth stitch). |
| **Round 6** | 1ch, 33sc (work 2sc in every fourth stitch). |
| **Rounds 7–10** | 1ch, 33sc. |
| **Round 11** | 1ch, 44sc (work 2sc in every third stitch). |
| **Round 12** | 1ch, 41sc (skip every 14th stitch of previous round). |
| **Round 13** | 1ch, 41sc. |
| **Round 14** | 1ch, 36sc (skip every eighth stitch). |
| **Round 15** | 1ch, 31sc (skip every seventh stitch). |
| **Round 16** | 1ch, 27sc (skip every seventh stitch). |
| **Rounds 17–18** | 1ch, 27sc. |
| **Round 19** | 1ch, 40sc (work 2sc in every second stitch of previous round). |
| **Round 20** | 1ch, 40sc. |

# CROCHET ANIMAL BASIC PROCESS

| Make eight body parts | Connect legs | Make body on top of legs | Add ears and nose to head. Sew eye. | Attach arms | Stuff body and head | Attach head to body |
|---|---|---|---|---|---|---|

## CONNECT THE LEGS

**SLIP KNOT**
Make a loop, insert the hook into the loop and wrap the yarn over the hook.

Draw up the loop to make it firm on the hook, but not too tight. Slip the loop off the hook.

Hold the two legs together and insert the hook through the middle stitch on each leg. Place the loop on the hook.

Draw loop through fabric. Wrap yarn around hook.

Draw the yarn through the loop.

Make 5sc through corresponding stitches on both legs.

Make 1ch and crochet the body as instructed on the following page.

## BODY

Beginning at one end of the seam, work 32sc into the stitches around the outside top edge of the legs.

At the end of each round of sc, ss into the first stitch. Work 14 rounds. Finish off and cut the yarn.

Insert the hook through the third stitch from right on the front of the body and make 10sc. Work three rows on these stitches.

Do the same for the back of the body. Leave a yarn tail about 8 in. each side.

## CHANGE COLOR

Finish a round, draw a loop of new color through the fabric, wrap yarn and pull through loop on hook to make a chain stitch.

Hold the tail of yarn close to the back of fabric and work single crochet over it with the new color.

## FINISHING YARN ENDS

When you finish the head, leave a yarn tail about 16 in. long. Use the tail to stitch the head onto the body.

Work the tails of the yarn into the fabric by using the hook to pull it through a few stitches.

## ATTACH ARMS

Use the tail of yarn from the body to sew the arms into the armholes on each side of body.

## STUFFING

Begin stuffing the body and head by pushing small amounts of stuffing into the ends of the legs and arms.

## NOSE

Sew a bead on as the nose, or work a nose in blanket stitch if the toy is for a baby. Insert stuffing and sew the nose to the face.

## EYE & EAR

Using contrasting yarn color and a sewing needle, make eyes in stem stitch. Sew ear to head, using the tail of the yarn.

## HEAD

With the tail of yarn at the back of the neck, stitch the head to the body at the neck openings.

When finished, pass the needle right through the neck to the other side before cutting off the yarn.

## MULTICOLOR YARN

Here's a chance to use up leftover yarn by tying short pieces together. Keep knots to the back of the fabric as you work.

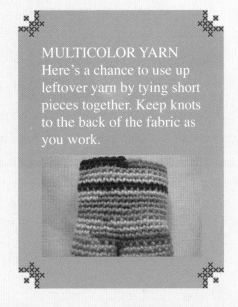

## FELTING BASIC PROCESS

| Two layers of wool laid at right angles | Wet with warm soapy water | Press down with hand | Massage with gentle to hard pressure | Roll in different directions and knead | Dip in hot and cold water | Allow to dry |
|---|---|---|---|---|---|---|

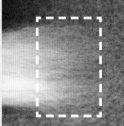
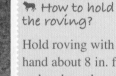

### 🐏 How to hold the roving?

Hold roving with left hand about 8 in. from end and gently pull out fibers with right hand.

### 🐏 How much overlap?

The dotted line, left, shows the overlap. It's important to draw the same amount of wool each time.

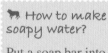

### 🐏 How to make soapy water?

Put a soap bar into warm water and roll it in your hand about 10 times for four cups of water.

### 🐏 How to sprinkle water?

Sprinkle by hand for small pieces. Pour water over the back of your hand so it spreads in droplets.

## SHEEP COAT

1. Cut a template (see page 56) from bubble wrap. Lay the fleece curls on the template, removing any seeds.

2. Lay two layers of wool roving on top of the curls, at right angles to each other. Allow 1½ in. to overhang the edge of the template.

3. Carefully sprinkle the whole piece with warm, soapy water, then pour warm, soapy water over the hand.

4. Press the piece with a soapy hand all over until it is evenly wet and all air bubbles have been removed.

5. Gently pat over the template for one minute, then add a little pressure to push out water and massage for three minutes.

6. Turn the whole piece over. Lay fleece curls on the template. Turn the overhanging ends of fibers over on top of the curls.

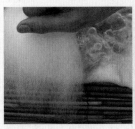   

7. Lay two layers of wool roving over the top, as before. Sprinkle the whole piece with warm soapy water.

8. Press then pat, gently tuck in wool that is overhanging the edge. Massage for three minutes as before.

9. Turn the piece and sprinkle more warm, soapy water. Massage on each side for 10 minutes, gradually increasing the pressure of your hands.

10. If the wool is getting cold, press out excess water and sprinkle with warm water. Continue massaging on both sides for 10 minutes.

11. When the fibers are well felted, cut the piece open along the base and remove the template. Put your hand inside and massage all over, especially along the joins. Turn the coat curly-side out and massage all over for five minutes. If curls do not attach firmly, turn the coat inside out, sprinkle with warm water and do more massaging.

12. Roll and knead the coat 50 times in your hands, then change direction and repeat the rolling and kneading 50 times.

13. Immerse alternately in warm and cold water and squeeze in each direction.

14. Press out excess water in a towel and manipulate coat, stretching and patting until the desired shape is formed.

15. Measure the position of the dog's arms and face, then use scissors to cut holes in the coat to correspond.

16. Cut the lower edge to a suitable length.

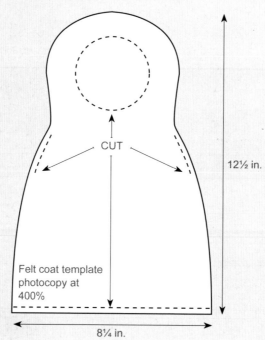

CUT

12½ in.

Felt coat template
photocopy at
400%

8¼ in.

## FIRST-TIME FELTMAKING  SOS

These tips from my experience may be useful for first-time feltmakers. Try making a small sample of felt at your kitchen sink and feel the fibers change in your palm.

☠ Problem 1: When you turn it over, the fibers start to come apart.

🐏 You need to massage more. Always pinch the fabric to test it before you move on to the next step: if you grasp single fibers, it needs more massaging. Make sure the water is pressed out of the fabric before you try to turn it.

☠ Problem 2: Ridges on the felt fabric.

🐏 Most ridges are formed when the fibers are moved by water pressure or your fingers as you massage. Be very gentle with the massage until the fabric passes the pinch test. Remove your rings, as these can catch the fibers.

☠ Problem 3: The edges of the fibers are spreading out as I massage.

🐏 Always massage from the outside edges towards the center.

☠ Problem 4: Folds form in the fabric around the edge of the template.

🐏 Your felt fabric is being stretched by the massage and is starting to bond with the fabric on the other side of the template. While you massage, pay attention to the edges of the template and keep massaging inward. It is hard to remove folds once they have formed.

☠ Problem 5: Holes in the felt fabric.

🐏 If you catch them before the felting process is complete, cut small pieces of wool roving about 1 in. long and place them over the hole. Use a small amount of soapy water and massage about three to five minutes.

If the felting process is already complete, rough up the surface with a needle, then do the same as above.

# Double dove bowl

The doves kiss and bring a moment of happiness and a pleasant mood into your room.

## Materials
Two different colors of wool roving; beads; embroidery thread

## Tools
Soap; bubble wrap; small bowl (diameter 4¾ in.); vanishing fabric marker; paper; sharp scissors; sewing needle

1. Cut a bowl template (see page 61) from bubble wrap.

2. Lay two layers of the first color of wool roving on top of the template at right angles to each other. Allow 1½ in. overhang around the edge of the template. See pages 54–57 for basic felting instructions.

3. Carefully sprinkle the whole piece with warm, soapy water.

4. Taking a bar of soap, gently rotate it in your wet hands. Press the wool all over with your soapy palms until it is evenly wet and no air bubbles are visible.

5. Soaping your hands frequently, pat gently over the template area only for about two minutes. Do not massage too much at this stage: if the felt gets too hard the fibers will not bond with the next layer.

6. Turn the whole piece over and fold the overhanging fibers inwards. Smooth any ridges out with your finger.

7. Place another two layers of wool roving (the first color) over the template as in Step 2 and repeat Steps 3–6.

8. Massage the folded edges to bond them to the base fabric, then massage the whole piece from the edges to the center for a minute.

9. Repeat Steps 2–8 using the second color of wool roving.

10. Massage with a bit more pressure, running a soapy hand over the surface in a light circular motion. If felt is getting cold, press out excess water with your palm and sprinkle with more warm soapy water. Massage the piece on each side for about 10 minutes.

11. Cut the top of the felted fabric and remove the template. With one hand inside, massage along the joins with the other hand to prevent a ridge forming.

12. Lay the piece on a flat surface with the joined edges in the center and continue with a firm massage for about five minutes. Roll and knead 50 times in one direction, then sprinkle with warm soapy water and roll and knead it 50 times in the opposite direction.

13. Immerse alternately in warm and cold water and squeeze in each direction.

14. Sprinkle with warm soapy water. Massage on both sides until all ridges are gone. Repeat Steps 13 and 14.

15. Press out in a towel to dry.

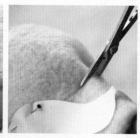

16. Place the small bowl inside the felt cup and pat the felt to fit the bowl shape. Allow the felt to dry with the bowl in place.

17. Trace a line around the top of the bowl onto the felt using vanishing fabric marker.

18. Cut out bird template and place it using the marked line as a guide. Trace the bird shape and cut out the bowl from the center.

19. Attach beads around the joined beaks using a sewing needle and embroidery thread.

## WOOD BEADS WOULD BE GOOD

The vivid colors and natural finish of wooden beads go well with the felt fabric.

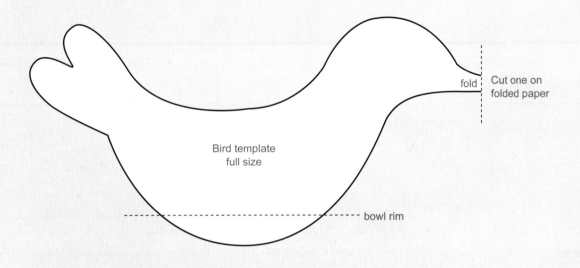

Cut one on
folded paper

fold

Bird template
full size

bowl rim

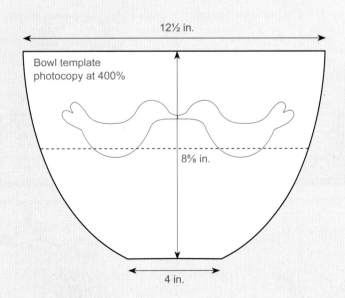

12½ in.

Bowl template
photocopy at 400%

8⅝ in.

4 in.

# Fluffy kitten

Fluffy kitten doesn't obey, but she always takes very nice care of you.

## Materials
Grey, white, pink, and red wool roving; small amount of fur

## Tools
Felting needle; sponge; needle and thread

### NEEDLE FELTING DEMONSTRATION

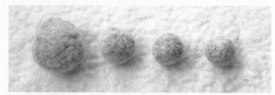

1 min    5 min    10 min    15 min

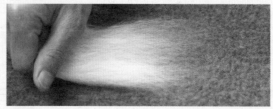

Hold the grey wool roving as shown above and gently draw off 10 pieces of wool for the head and seven pieces for the body. More wool may be required if the fibers are shorter.

## HEAD

1. Roll the wool between your palms to make a round ball of fiber.

2. Hold ball in hand and poke the top with a felting needle until it is flat. Rotate ball and continue for 15 minutes to get a small ball.

## BODY

1. Work as for the head (Steps 1 and 2), but stop after about 10 minutes and roll between your palms to make an oval shape.

2. Poke the needle into the top and bottom of the oval to flatten the ends, forming a nice body shape.

## FACE

1. Poke a circle around the center of the face to make a nose. Poke a little more from the sides and top to make a firm shape.

2. Draw a little white wool from the roving and flatten it. Place it on the nose and poke with the felting needle until it is firm.

3. Take a little pink wool on your finger and flatten it on the tip of the nose. Poke to make a triangle.

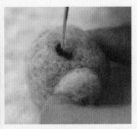

4. Take a little red wool on your finger and roll it. Cut it to about ¼ in., lay it in place and poke to attach it in a crescent shape.

## EARS

 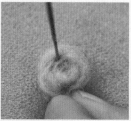  

1. Draw a little grey wool from roving, hold one end and roll twice to create a small round shape.

2. Holding both free ends of the fibers, place the shape on sponge and poke it in a circular pattern until it is flat. Turn it over and repeat.

3. Roll one end with your fingers to make it pointed. Continue poking until you have a triangle shape.

4. Leave about ⅜ in. of loose fibers for attaching to head.

## ARMS, LEGS & TAIL

1. Draw a little grey wool from the roving. Continue pulling fibers apart from both ends to make them shorter, until they are about 2–2½ in. long.

2. Fold the wool in half, place it on the sponge and poke until the felt is quite hard. Turn it over and repeat.

3. Roll the felt piece between your fingers to make the desired shape.

4. Poke on the end to make a rounded shape. Be careful not to poke your finger!

## ATTACH LIMBS

   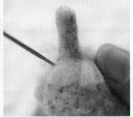

1. Pick up a few fibers from the base of the head and the top of the body.

2. Hold the head and body together and use the felting needle to poke the fibers you picked up to the inside.

3. Spread out the unfelted wool at the end of the ears and limbs in a circle, and trim it back to ⅜ in. long.

4. Hold the limb in place and use the felting needle to poke the fibers into the body.

## FINISHING

1. When all limbs are attached, poke around the neck to shape it. More poking will reduce the size. If you find that the piercings remain visible, pat with your fingers.

2. Use the felting needle to poke a straight line from the pink triangle down the center of the nose. Add a fluffy collar if desired and stitch in place.

### ABOUT BALANCE

When you make needle-felted animals, balance is important. This kitten's big head and tiny body are what make her so cute. Change the thickness of the arms and legs to make the kitten look different. Make the arms and legs smaller by poking them more with the felting needle.

# Nirvana rabbit

Small felt animals need delicate fingerwork. As you work, imagine your finished rabbit in your mind or, if you are making a present for someone, imagine their smiling face.

## Materials
Orange, red, pink wool roving; yellow and red embroidery thread; yellow felt fabric; fiberfill stuffing

## Tools
Soap; bubble wrap; sewing needle

### TIPS FOR SMALL FELTED ITEMS

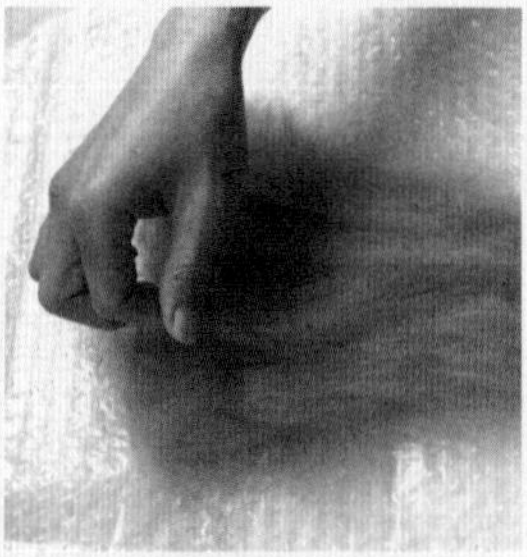

**Small projects.** Wool must be drawn out little by little from the roving and laid evenly over the template.

### HEAD, ARMS, LEGS, BODY

1. Cut templates (see page 69) from bubble wrap. Lay two layers of wool on top of the template at right angles to each other, allowing 1¼ in. of fiber to overhang the edges of the template.

 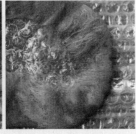

2. Pat the wool gently to flatten the fibers and carefully pull the template from under the wool.

3. Carefully sprinkle the center of the wool (don't wet the edges) with warm soapy water, then lay the template on the center and press down gently with fingertips to push out any air bubbles.

4. Fold the edges of the wool inwards over the template. Cut between the ears if it is difficult to fold the fibers. Sprinkle with soapy water and pat it with your finger to make it flat.

5. Fill in the center of the template with two layers of the wool as before. Sprinkle with warm soapy water and press gently all over with your fingers.

6. Soaping your hands frequently, pat the piece gently with your fingers for three minutes. Tuck in any loose wool fibers.

7. Turn the whole piece over and massage with soapy hands for three minutes.

8. Knead gently in warm water. Remove from water and massage with soapy hands, 10 minutes each side. If it gets cold, press out water, sprinkle with warm, soapy water and keep massaging.

9. Cut where indicated and remove the template. Put your finger inside and pat all over, especially massaging along the join with your other finger to prevent ridges forming. Turn inside out and massage all over for about five minutes.

10. Immerse alternately in warm and cold water and squeeze in each direction.

11. Pinch the felt between your fingertips: if you can lift single fibers from the felt easily, it needs more massage.

12. Press out in a towel to dry and pat for a flat surface. Allow the felt to dry.

FACE            ASSEMBLY

Make eyes with stem stitch. Cut out a heart shape from a piece of yellow felt and stitch it in place. Stitch around the ears too.

1. Cut the arms and legs at an angle so they will lie along the body.

2. Stuff all body parts through the openings.

3. Use red thread to stitch the head, arms and legs to the body. Attach the left hand to the cheek to make a meditative posture.

Nirvana rabbit head template
Photocopy all pieces at 400%

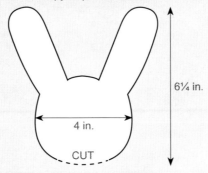

6¼ in.

4 in.

CUT

Nirvana rabbit body template

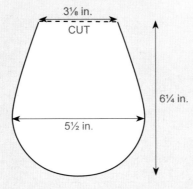

3⅛ in.

CUT

6¼ in.

5½ in.

Nirvana rabbit leg template

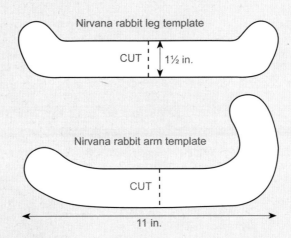

CUT    1½ in.

Nirvana rabbit arm template

CUT

11 in.

# Wiener dog draft stopper

Mother is not interested in herself. She is always thinking about her baby, and they will have sweet dreams together in vivid color.

## Materials
Cotton canvas fabric; red felt fabric; red embroidery thread; fiberfill stuffing; door draft stopper; red acrylic paint

## Tools
Paper for template; needle; neutral sewing thread; vanishing fabric marker

1. Make a template using the diagram on page 73, then cut it in the middle and add more paper so the total length is 36 in. or the length of your door draft stopper. Make a template for the baby using the diagram on page 72. Trace onto canvas and cut two bodies and eight legs.

2. Cut out the felt shapes. Cut two ears and eight pattern shapes for the mother, and two ears and three pattern shapes for the baby.

## PROCESS

Cut out all pieces ▶ Stitch all decoration on body ▶ Sew legs and turn to right side ▶ Place legs on body ▶ Stitch around body ▶ Stuff nose and tail; insert draft stopper ▶ Sew up tail opening and paint nose

3. Arrange the felt pieces on the body and mark their positions with vanishing fabric marker.

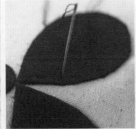

4. Stitch the felt shapes in place on the body and use stem stitch to make an eye.

5. With right sides together, match the legs in pairs and stitch around the edges.

6. Turn them to the right side and attach them to the body as shown in the top diagram on page 72.

7. Stitch around the body, leaving an opening at the tail.

8. Turn to the right side and stuff the nose and tail with stuffing. Use a stick to poke it in.

9. Insert the draft stopper or stuffing and stitch up the opening in the tail. Paint the nose with acrylic paint.

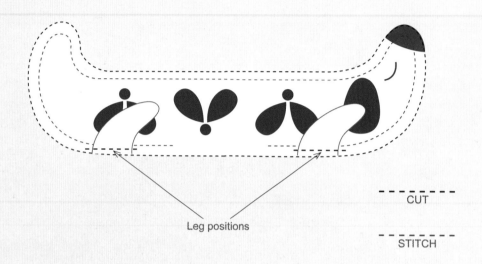

Leg positions

- - - - CUT

- - - - STITCH

Baby dog template
photocopy at 250%

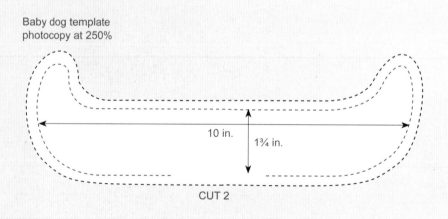

10 in.

1¾ in.

CUT 2

CUT 8

1⅜ in.

CUT 2    CUT 3

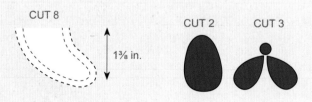

Mother dog template
photocopy at 400%

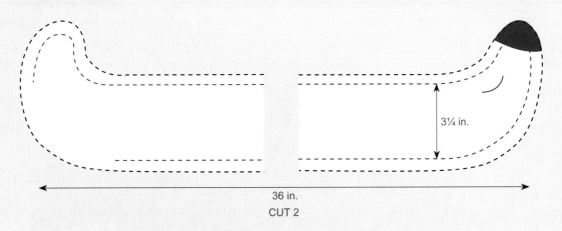

36 in.
CUT 2

3¼ in.

CUT 8

2¾ in.

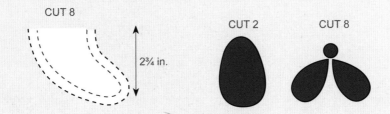

CUT 2     CUT 8

# Whispering rabbits ring holder

Three little rabbits will keep your jewelry safe while you sleep. They will not wake you as they whisper their secrets.

## Materials
White wool roving, beads or crystals on chain; fiberfill stuffing; white felt fabric

## Tools
Soap; bubble wrap; sewing needle; sewing thread

1. Cut a rabbit template from bubble wrap using the diagram on page 77. Lay two layers of wool on top of the template at right angles to each other, allowing 1¼ in. of fiber to overhang the edges of the template. See pages 54–57 for basic felting instructions.

2. Pat the wool gently to flatten the fibers and press the layers together. Carefully pull the template from under the wool.

3. Carefully sprinkle the center of the wool pile (don't wet the edges) with warm soapy water, then lay the

template on the center and press down gently with fingertips to push out any air bubbles.

4. Fold the overhanging edges of the wool inwards over the template, sprinkle with soapy water and pat it with your finger to make it flat.

5. Fill in the center of the template with two layers of the wool as before. Sprinkle with warm soapy water and press gently all over with your fingers.

6. Soaping your hands frequently, pat the piece gently with your fingers for three minutes. Tuck in any loose wool fibers.

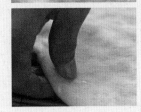

7. Turn the whole piece over and massage with soapy hands for three minutes.

8. Knead gently in warm water. Remove it from the water and massage with soapy hands for about 10 minutes each side. If the wool is getting cold, press out excess water, sprinkle with warm, soapy water and keep massaging.

9. Cut a 1½ in. slit in the bottom and remove the template. Put your finger inside and pat all over, especially massaging along the join with your other finger to prevent ridges forming. Turn inside out and massage all over for about five minutes.

10. Immerse alternately in warm and cold water and squeeze in each direction.

11. Pinch the felt between your fingertips: if you can lift single fibers from the felt easily, it needs more massage.

12. Press out in a towel to dry and pat to get a flat surface. Put stuffing inside and allow the felt to dry.

## TAIL

## FINISH

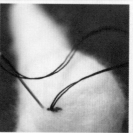

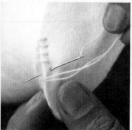

1. Cut three ¾ in. pieces of wool roving, tease it out with your fingers and roll it between your palms to make a ball.

2. Wet your hands with warm soapy water and roll it very softly at first, gradually applying more pressure until it is felted.

1. Sew eyes with red thread and stem stitch. Sew the felted tail in place.

2. Level the base and cut an oval shape from a flat piece of felt fabric. Stitch in place, then add chain and beads to the ear.

## FLOWER BASE

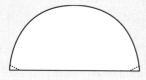

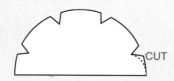

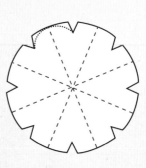

1. Lay down two layers of white wool roving (8 in. x 8 in.) to make a small piece of felt. Follow the felting instructions on page 99.

2. Cut a 5½ in. diameter circle. Fold it in half and cut a ³/₈ in. notch from the corners of the flat edge.

3. Open and refold the circle, matching the notches at the top. Cut corner notches as in Step 2. Repeat another two times until you have eight equal petals.

4. Round off the corners of the petals as shown in the diagram above. Sew rabbits to the flower base for stability.

Rabbit template
full size

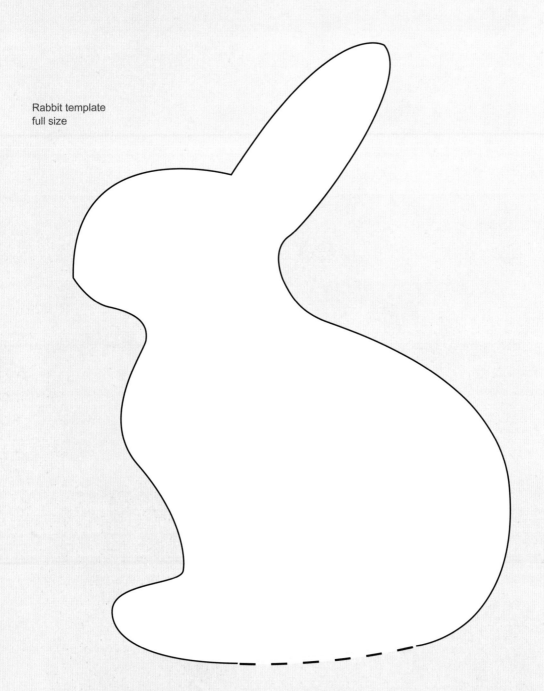

# Masked cat cushion

This introvert cat hides his strong heart and brave thinking behind a mask.

## Materials
White and natural grey wool roving; white yarn; black felt; fine black yarn; stuffing

## Tools
Soap; bubble wrap; wool needle; size J crochet hook

### PRE-FELT

1. Cut a bubble wrap template 18½ x 24 in., rounding the corners. Lay two layers of white wool roving at right angles to each other. Sprinkle with warm, soapy water and press gently until evenly wet and air bubbles are pressed out.

2. Soap your hands and gently massage the surface for a minute. Resoaping your hands frequently, use a little more pressure and massage for three minutes. Use your fingers to firm the edge.

3. Turn the piece over and repeat Step 2.

4. Rinse gently in warm water and allow the pre-felt to dry. Cut out the cat shape using the template on page 81.

## CAT CUSHION

1. Place the cat-shaped pre-felt piece on the center of the template. Lay three layers of natural grey wool roving over the top of the pre- 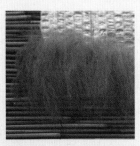 felt shape, at right angles to each other, allowing 1½ in. overhang around the template's edge.

2. Pat the wool to settle it down and carefully sprinkle warm soapy water all over.

3. Press the wool all over with wet, soapy hands until it is evenly wet and the air bubbles are pressed out.

4. Soaping your hands frequently, massage gently for one minute. Use a little more pressure to push the water out and massage only over the template area for five minutes.

5. Turn the whole piece over and fold the overhanging fibers inwards over the bubble wrap. Ensure that no ridges form in the folded fibers, by smoothing them out with your soapy fingers.

6. Arrange three layers of wool on top of the bubble wrap, at right angles to each other as before, allowing 1½ in. overhang around the template's edge. Repeat Steps 2–4.

7. Turn the whole piece over and fold the overhanging edges inwards. Sprinkle with a little warm soapy water and massage on both sides about 10 minutes, taking care around the edges.

8. Gently knead the felt in warm water. Lay it on a flat surface, sprinkle with warm, soapy water, then roll and knead it 50 times in one direction. Unroll, sprinkle with warm, soapy water and roll and knead 50 times in the opposite direction.

9. Cut an 8 in. slit in the bottom edge and remove the template. Put your hand

inside the cushion and massage all over with soapy hands for about five minutes, especially along the joins, to prevent ridges forming. Turn right-side out and massage all over about five minutes to make sure the pre-felt is bonded to the cushion fabric.

10. Immerse alternately in warm and cold water and squeeze in each direction.

11. Repeat the massaging and kneading from Steps 7–8 using stronger pressure.

12. Pinch the felt between your fingertips: if you can lift single fibers from the felt easily, it needs more massage.

13. Press out water in a towel to dry and pat firmly to create a flat surface.

14. Allow the felt to dry completely before embellishing the cat's face and stuffing the cushion, below.

## FINISHING

1. Cut black felt to mask shape using the template opposite. Stitch the mask onto the face with black yarn.

2. Embroider the eyeballs, nose and mouth with fine black yarn. Stuff the cushion to the desired firmness.

3. Using a bulky white yarn, stitch around the edge, including across the opening at the bottom, using blanket stitch.

4. Make blanket stitches $^3/_8$ in. apart. Work one single crochet (see page 49) in the top of each blanket stitch.

Introvert cat template
photocopy at 320%

21 in.

9½ in.

# Gentle owl necklace holder

Owl sisters always wear a smile on their face. Even when they are sad, the sisters keep smiling—this is the way to create happiness.

## Materials
Cotton canvas; acrylic paint; small piece of ribbon; fiberfill stuffing

## Tools
Paintbrushes (fine point and flat); sewing needle and thread; pencil or vanishing fabric marker; fine-tip black permanent fabric marker or waterproof marker

1. Make a template using the diagram on page 84. Trace the shape on the canvas. Draw the ³⁄₈ in. seam allowance freehand.

2. Mix up acrylic paint in a color of your choice and add a little water. Too much water will cause the paint to bleed into the fabric.

3. On one owl shape, paint the outline first, then fill in the colored area with a flat brush.

4. Allow to dry overnight. Cut out both shapes and lay the painted front face-up on a flat surface.

5. Fold ribbon in half and lay it on the point of the head, raw edges together. Baste in place inside seam line.

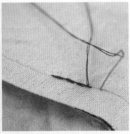

6. Lay the two bird shapes with right sides together and sew around the traced line. Leave a gap at the base.

7. Clip curves of the seam allowance to prevent puckering, and turn the owl right-side out.

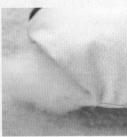

8. Insert small amounts of stuffing until the owl is as firm as you like.

9. Sew up the opening in the base.

10. Draw on the eyes and the beak using a black marker.

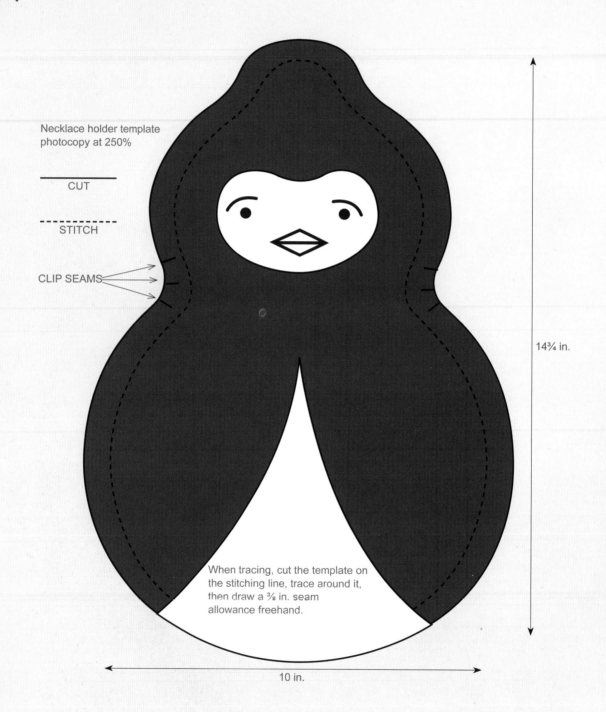

Necklace holder template
photocopy at 250%

———————— CUT

------------ STITCH

CLIP SEAMS

When tracing, cut the template on
the stitching line, trace around it,
then draw a ⅜ in. seam
allowance freehand.

14¾ in.

10 in.

Change the color to suit your feeling,
and the face to suit your mood!

# Poodle baby boots

Make these first boots with fluffy poodle ears for a newborn baby.
To make the poodle ears and beaded nose, you need delicacy, so do
it slowly.

## Materials
Beige wool roving; white mohair yarn;
white pearl cotton thread; pearl beads

## Tools
Soap; bubble wrap; size C crochet hook;
size 4 steel crochet hook; sewing needle
and thread

BABY BOOTIES

1. Cut a template (see opposite) from bubble
   wrap. Lay two layers of wool on top of
   the template at right angles to each other,
   allowing 1¼ in. of fiber to overhang the
   edges.

2. Follow the felting instructions for the
   Nirvana rabbit on page 67, Steps 2–10.

3. Turn the boots to the right side and
   massage all over with soapy hands for
   about five minutes. Repeat Step 10.

4. Pinch the felt between your fingertips:
   if you can lift single fibers from the felt
   easily, it needs more massage.

5. Press out in a towel to dry. Pat firmly to make a flat surface and pull the fabric to form the boot into the desired shape. Allow the felt to dry.

6. Trim the top edge to make it even. Make the fluffy top and ear and beaded nose for the boots (see next page) and attach with sewing needle and thread.

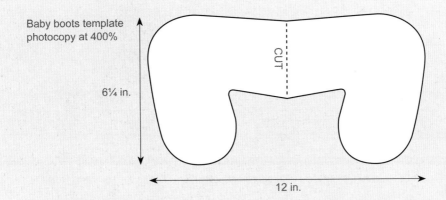

Baby boots template
photocopy at 400%

CUT

6¼ in.

12 in.

## FLUFFY TOP (Use mohair yarn and size C crochet hook.)

 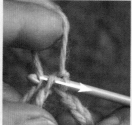  

Make 30 chain, or enough to fit the top of the boot, slip stitch to form a loop. See pages 48–49 for basic crochet instructions.

**LOOP SINGLE CROCHET** Make one chain, hold a loop of yarn with two fingers and insert the hook into the next stitch.

Wrap the yarn over the hook and draw it through the stitch, leaving the loop on the outside then complete a single crochet.

Make four rows of loop stitch. Sew the loopy fringe to the top of the boot.

## EAR

Make a double loop to begin and work 10 loop single crochet as above, in the circle. Pull the yarn tail tight then make a circle (see pages 48–49).

**Round 2** Work loop single crochet, increase by making two stitches in every third stitch.
**Round 3** Work loop stitch, increase every second stitch.

Fold the ear in half and crochet the two sides together with three slip stitches.

Cut the yarn then draw the tail through the loop. Pull the yarn firmly. Pull the beginning of the yarn through to the wrong side and knot the tails together.

NOSE

 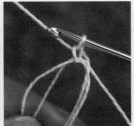  

String 60 beads onto the pearl cotton. You will slide a bead up the yarn and work over it to create each beaded single crochet (bsc).

Using the size 4 steel crochet hook, take the beginning of the pearl cotton and make a double ring to begin, as on pages 48–49.

Slide a bead up the yarn, put the hook through the double loop, wrap the yarn over the hook and draw it through the double loop.

Wrap the yarn over the hook and draw it through two loops on the hook to complete a single crochet.

Slide a bead up the yarn for each stitch. Make 10sc in the loop, with a bead in each one.

Pull the yarn tail until one loop begins to tighten, then pull the tight loop to adjust the other loop, then pull the tail until both loops are tight.

**Round 1**  10bsc as shown at left, turn work and continue from Round 2 in opposite direction.

**Round 2**  1ch, 15bsc (work 2bsc in same stitch in every second stitch of the previous row).

**Round 3**  1ch, 20bsc (work 2bsc in every third stitch).

**Round 4**  1ch, 15bsc (skip every fourth stitch).

**Round 5**  1ch, 10sc with no beads (skip every third stitch).

Finish off, working the end of the yarn into the back of the work.

# Bird tent

A hanging tent holds a smile for everybody. With a swinging bird inside, it brings you a little happiness every day.

## Materials
Orange, white, yellow, and black wool roving; beads or twig and thread for feet; chain or metallic thread; short length of ribbon; fine yarn for rug

## Tools
Soap; bubble wrap; vanishing fabric marker; felting needle; sponge; size C crochet hook; sewing needle and thread

TENT

1. Cut a template (see page 93) from bubble wrap. Follow Steps 2–10 on pages 58–59 to make the felt tent.

2. Draw the shape of the entrance with vanishing fabric marker. Cut the entrance, remove the template and massage the felt along the joins until all ridges are gone. Continue with Steps 12–15 from page 59. Pat firmly to form the desired egg shape.

# BIRD

1. Draw pieces of yellow wool from the roving about 13 times and roll between palms to make a ball.

2. Hold ball in hand and poke the top with a felting needle until it is flat. Rotate ball and continue to get a small ball.

3. After 10 minutes of poking with the felting needle, roll the body between your palms to make an oval shape.

4. To make the head, poke felting needle in a circle as in the picture. Poke the head more to make it smaller.

## TAIL　　　　WINGS　　　　BEAK

 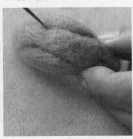  

Spread the tail end on a firm sponge. Poke two lines to flatten and into the end to round.

On the sides of the body, poke curved lines to outline the wings.

1. Take a small piece of orange roving and roll three times. Poke with felting needle until flat.

2. Roll to a point at one end to make a cone, attach it to the face, then poke to get a beak shape.

## EYE

## FEET

1. Take a little white wool on your finger and roll it into a circle. Put it in position and poke around the outer edge to attach it.

2. Take a smaller amount of black wool on your finger, roll it into a small circle and poke it into the center of the white eye circle.

Sew on two beads and attach a small twig perch with orange pearl cotton thread.

## FINISH

1. Cut a slit in the top of the tent for the ribbon and stitch the ends of the ribbon in place inside the tent.

2. Cut a length of chain to the desired size (about 3½ in. depending on size of tent) and attach a jump ring at each end.

3. Stitch one jump ring to the bird's back. Attach the other end of the chain inside the top of the tent.

4. Roll up the door and use pearl cotton thread or fine yarn to tie it up in two places.

## RUG

See basic crochet instructions on pages 48–49. Make a ring to begin.

**Round 1**  10sc
**Round 2**  1ch, 15sc (work 2sc in same stitch in every second stitch of previous round).
**Round 3**  1ch, 20sc (work 2sc in every third stitch).
**Round 4**  1ch, 26sc (work 2sc in every third stitch).
**Round 5**  1ch, 26sc
**Round 6**  1ch, 34sc (work 2sc in every third stitch).
**Round 7**  1ch, 51sc (work 2sc in every second stitch).
**Round 8**  1ch, 51sc
**Round 9**  1ch, 57sc (work 2sc in every eighth stitch).

Finish off and work yarn tails into fabric. Place inside the tent.

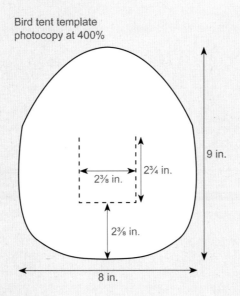

Bird tent template
photocopy at 400%

2⅜ in.

2¾ in.

9 in.

2⅜ in.

8 in.

# Donkey mother and child

If you make a needle-felted mother and baby donkey, they carry a fragrant burden and bring best wishes from your heart.

**Materials**
Grey, black, and white wool roving;
two 6 in. pipe cleaners (mother);
two 4 in. pipe cleaners (baby)

**Tools**
Felting needle; firm sponge

### HEAD & NECK

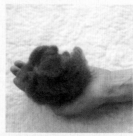 

1. Draw pieces of grey wool from the roving about 10 times and roll between your palms to make a ball.

2. Hold ball in hand and poke the top with a felting needle until it is flat. Rotate ball and continue for ten minutes.

3. Roll the ball between your palms to elongate it.

4. Make a head by bending one third of the length and poking the felting needle along the bend to shape.

5. To make the head and neck thinner, squeeze the wool and poke with the felting needle from different directions.

6. Keep poking until the wool is firm and good shape. Pick up a few fibers from base of the neck to attach to the body.

## BODY & LEGS

1. Twist pipe cleaners together as shown, about 2³/₈ in. for the mother and 2 in. for the baby.

2. Roll wool around the twisted section in different directions, making three layers. Poke to make a firm body.

3. Fold wool vertically over leg and poke ends into body. Wrap more wool around and poke ends into body.

4. Hold the leg between two fingers and poke to create a firm shape.

## TAIL

   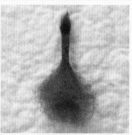

1. Draw a little black wool from roving. Continue pulling fibers apart from both ends to make them shorter, about 2–2³/₈ in. long.

2. Take a little wool from grey roving and put black wool on top as shown. Roll the grey wool between your fingers.

3. Place the wool on the sponge and poke it with the felting needle. Continue poking and rolling it until it is firm.

4. Loosen a few fibers at the end that will join to the body.

## EAR

1. Pull a little grey wool from roving and fold in half.

2. Lay it on the sponge and poke until it gets hard. Turn it over and do the other side. Roll one end with your fingers to make it pointed.

3. Take a little white wool on your finger and form it into an oval shape.

4. Put it on the ear and use the felting needle to outline a leaf shape. Poke until it is flat and bonded to the base.

## EYE

## FEET

1. Take a little white wool on your finger make it round and flat. Place on the face and outline an almond shape, then poke until it is flat.

2. Add a small amount of black wool for the iris.

3. Join the head to the body, holding it in place and poking the loose fibers in to body. Join the tail in the same manner.

Take a little black wool, roll it around the feet and poke it in to make the hooves.

## FINISHING

When all limbs are attached, poke a little more around the nose to shape it. If the felting needle leaves visible holes, pat with fingers to cover them.

**TAKE YOUR TIME** Continue poking all over until you create a pleasing body shape.

# Chick-cat blanket

Imagine a fluffy chick's body with a cat's head — it's really cute and really clever. It sits on the cloud to get away from the rain.

**Materials**
Natural grey, orange, yellow, pale blue, and white wool roving; black, orange, yellow, and pale blue fine yarn

**Tools**
Soap; bubble wrap; sewing needle; watering can

1. Using orange, yellow and pale blue wool, lay two layers of wool roving at right angles to each other, covering an area 9 x 11½ in. Make a pre-felt sheet, following the instructions on page 78.

2. Using white wool, make a pre-felt sheet 11½ x 18¼ in.

3. Cut out chick-cats, rain drops, flowers and clouds from pre-felt, using templates on pages 100–101.

## BLANKET

1. Cut a 30 x 42 in. piece of bubble wrap and lay it on a table. Place the pre-felt cut-outs on the bubble wrap in position. Using natural grey wool, lay three layers of wool at right angles to each other. Carefully sprinkle the whole with warm soapy water (use a watering can), press the wool all over until it is evenly wet and the air bubbles are pressed out.

2. Soaping hands frequently, gently massage all over. After a few minutes, add a little pressure to push out excess water and massage for five minutes.

3. Use a soapy finger to rub the surface in a circular motion at the edges. If the wool is getting cold, press out excess water and sprinkle with more warm water. Massage all over for a further 10 minutes.

4. Roll the bubble wrap to turn the whole piece over, remove the template and repeat Steps 2–3.

5. Roll the blanket, put it in warm water and knead gently. Return it to the table and sprinkle with more warm soapy water. Roll and knead 50 times in one direction, then unroll and sprinkle with more soapy water. Roll and knead 50 times in the opposite direction.

6. Immerse alternately in warm and cold water and squeeze in each direction.

7. Repeat Step 3, using stronger pressure.

8. Pinch the felt between your fingertips: if you can lift single fibers from the felt easily, it needs more massage.

9. Press out in a bath towel to dry and pat the surface flat. Allow to dry.

10. Sew eyes, nose, mouth with fine yarn. Match the yarn for the feet with the color of the body.

Proposal from Chick-cat

Make pre-felt the day before you start to make the blanket.

Chick-cat diagram
photocopy at 200%

8¾ in.

Rainy day diagram
photocopy at 200%

# Winking cat tea cozy

This teapot warmer always gets lots of attention when teatime comes. Its winking face will put a happy flavor in your tea.

## Materials
Brown, beige, and yellow wool roving; yellow fine yarn; yellow felt; beads

## Tools
Soap; bubble wrap; sewing needle

1. Cut a template from bubble wrap, using the diagram on page 105.

2. Randomly arrange a small amount of brown wool on the template. Place two layers of beige wool over the brown, at right angles to each other. Allow 1¼ in. overhang at the edges of the template.

3. Carefully sprinkle the whole piece with warm, soapy water. With soapy hands, press wool all over until it is evenly wet and the air bubbles are pressed out.

4. Soaping your hands frequently, pat the wool gently over the area of the template for three minutes.

5. Turn the whole piece over. Arrange a small amount of brown wool on the template. Fold the overhanging ends of the fiber inwards. If ridges form in the folded fibers, smooth them out with a soapy finger.

6 Lay two layers of beige wool at right angles to each other, allow 1¼ in. overhang at the edges of the template.

7. Repeat Steps 3–5. Massage with a bit more pressure, running your hand over the surface in a light circular motion. If the wool is getting cold, press out excess water and sprinkle with warm soapy water. Massage 10 minutes each side.

8. Cut across the bottom edge, remove the template and insert one hand inside. Massage along the join with your other hand to prevent a ridge forming.

9. Lay the inside-out cozy on a flat surface with the join centered and massage strongly for about five minutes. Roll and knead 50 times in one direction. Unroll, sprinkle with warm soapy water and roll it in the opposite direction 50 times. Turn right-side out and repeat Step 9.

10. Immerse alternately in warm and cold water and squeeze in each direction.

11. Pinch the felt between your fingertips: if you can lift single fibers from the felt easily, it needs more massage.

12. Press out in a towel to dry. Pat and pull the tea cozy to get the desired shape.

## FELT BALL

1. Cut four ¾ in. pieces of wool roving, tease the fibers out with your fingers and roll between your palms to make a ball.

2. Wet hands with warm, soapy water, roll gently at first then increase pressure.

3. Soak the ball in warm soapy water and roll hard until you get a smooth finish.

## EAR

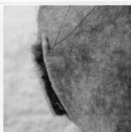

## EYE

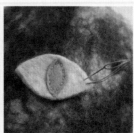

Measure the cozy on your teapot and cut slits for the handle and spout. Trim the base to table level.

1. Use the leftover felt for the ears and eyes. Cut out ears (see template opposite) and stitch around the edge.

2. Cut a 2³/₈ in. slit and slip the base of the ear through. Turn the cozy inside out and stitch the ear in place.

1. Cut an eye out of felt leftovers and an iris out of yellow felt and sew the iris in place, then sew the eye on the tea cozy.

## FINISH

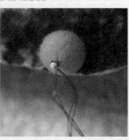

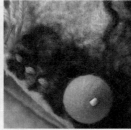

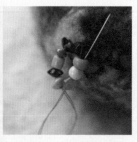

2. Cut a winking eye out of felt leftovers and sew it in place.

1. Attach the felt ball paws at the front of the cozy, using a bead to anchor.

2. Work running stitch around the bottom edge of the tea cozy with yellow yarn.

3. Make a loop of beads and sew them to the top of the tea cozy as a handle.

Cat tea cozy template
photocopy at 400%

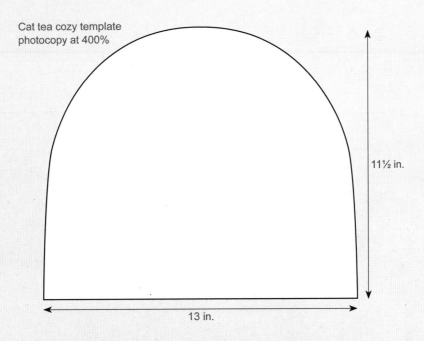

11½ in.

13 in.

Cat tea cozy
ear and eye templates
photocopy at 400%

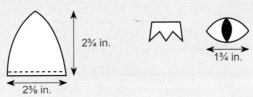

2¾ in.

2⅜ in.

1¾ in.

# Tiny bunny pillow

After hard work, take a catnap at your desk. Lay your cheek on the soft, fleecy bunny for a little smiling time.

## Materials
White, pink wool roving; raw fleece kid curls; black and pink ready-made felt sheet; fine white yarn; fiberfill stuffing

## Tools
Soap; bubble wrap; scrap of cardboard; sewing needle and thread

CURLY FELT SHEET

1. Remove any seeds or foreign matter from the kid curls and lay the curls on a sheet of bubble wrap, covering an area of 10 x 12 in.

2. On top of the curls, place pieces of pink wool roving then lay two layers of white wool roving at right angles to each other.

3. Carefully sprinkle the whole piece with warm, soapy water.

4. Gently soap your wet hands. Press the wool all over with flat hands until it is evenly wet and the air bubbles are pressed out.

5. Soaping your hands frequently, make light circular motions over the surface of the wool for about three minutes, then add a little pressure to push out excess water and massage for about 10 minutes.

6. Turn the whole piece over and massage about five minutes.

7. Immerse in warm water and knead gently. Remove it from the water and roll and knead it 50 times in one direction, then roll and knead it 50 times in the opposite direction.

8. Immerse alternately in warm and cold water and squeeze in each direction.

9. Press out in a towel to dry and pat the surface flat. Allow the felt to dry.

## POM-POM TAIL

1. Cut a piece of cardboard 1¼ in. wide and wind the fine white yarn around 60 times.

2. Slip the loop off the cardboard, wrap yarn around the center of the loops and tie a tight knot.

3. Cut the loops and fluff out the yarn to make a ball.

4. Cut away about half the length of the yarn, then trim to a neat, round shape.

## BUNNY PILLOW

 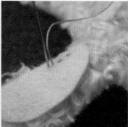 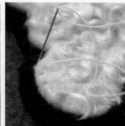 

1. Cut the bunny shape from the pink kid curls felt using the template 2, opposite.

2. Cut the inner ears from pink felt and sew them onto the front of the shape.

3. Cut two bunny shapes from black felt using template 1. Sew the kid curls felt shape to a black one.

4. Sew the black shapes together using blanket stitch, leaving a small opening for stuffing.

 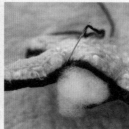 

5. Attach the pom-pom tail and secure with a few stitches.

6. Push small amounts of stuffing into the ears and legs, then stuff the shape firmly and sew up the opening.

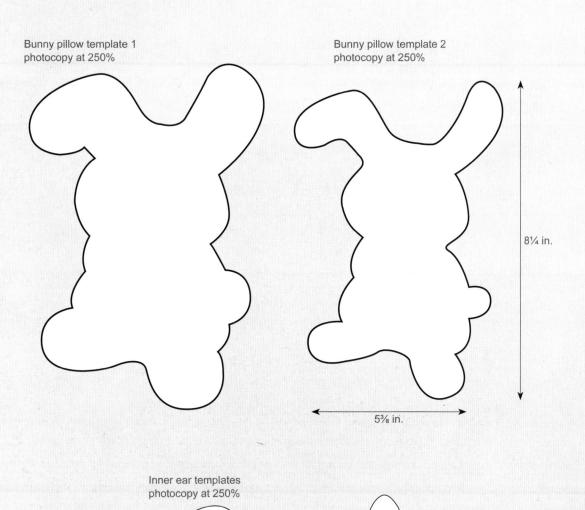

Bunny pillow template 1
photocopy at 250%

Bunny pillow template 2
photocopy at 250%

8¼ in.

5⅜ in.

Inner ear templates
photocopy at 250%

# Pair of bears

Make two bears in different colors and melt one into the other.
A warm hug is a quick way to relax.

**Materials**
Natural grey, white wool roving

**Tools**
Felting needle; sponge; sewing needle
and thread

1. Draw pieces of wool from the roving
   about 13 times and roll it between your
   palms to make a ball.

2. Hold the ball in your hand and poke the
   top with a felting needle until it is flat.
   Rotate ball and continue for 15 minutes
   to get a small ball.

3. Roll the ball between your palms to make
   a longer shape.

4. Poke the felting needle around the ends of
   the shape to round them.

5. Poke the felting needle around the
   neckline to form a head and body. Hold
   the head firmly between your fingers and
   poke to create the shape.

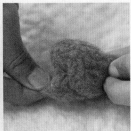

6. Hold the body upside down and poke in a line across the end to divide into two legs.

7. Pull legs to make them longer. Hold leg between two fingers and poke in all directions to form the shape.

8. Stretch the body a little by pulling it with your fingers poke in a line across the neck and nose.

9. Make ears and arms, following the instructions given for the fluffy kitten on page 64.

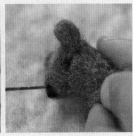

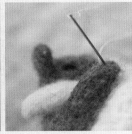

10. Attach ears and arms to head and body following instructions given for the fluffy kitten on page 65.

11. Take a little wool on your finger and poke it into place to create the nose and eyes. See page 63.

12. Gently hold the body to make a curved back, then poke it. Sew each bear's hands to the other's body.

13. Pass needle through the body to the other side before cutting off the yarn. Squeeze bears together to shape.

# Shy reindeer toy

Going to an important meeting, he gets nervous. Shyness is just one of his qualities.

## Materials
Jute yarn; white fluffy yarn; red lace-weight yarn; fiberfill stuffing

## Tools
Size C crochet hook; size 4 steel crochet hook; sewing needle; cardboard

Use the same pattern as for the black dog on pages 48–53: only the ears and horns are different.

### BODY
Connect the two legs and work the body as for the black dog, or make a bigger tummy:

| | |
|---|---|
| **Round 1** | 1ch, 36sc |
| **Round 2** | 1ch, 43sc (work 2sc in same stitch, every fourth stitch of previous row). |
| **Round 3** | 1ch, 49sc (work 2sc in every seventh stitch). |
| **Rounds 4–5** | 1ch, 49sc |
| **Round 6** | 1ch, 43sc (skip every seventh stitch). |
| **Round 7** | 1ch, 36sc (skip every fourth stitch). |
| **Rounds 8–14** | 36sc |

## HORNS

1. Make two short horns using red yarn and steel crochet hook. Begin with 10sc in a ring, as on pages 48–49.

2. Join horns with seven slip stitches.

3. Make one chain and work 14sc around the outer edge. Work 10 rows of single crochet.

4. Alternatively, you could make one short horn and one long horn and stitch the short horn to the longer one.

### SHORT HORNS
**Round 1**     1ch, 10sc
**Round 2**     1ch, 12sc (work 2sc in same stitch in every fourth stitch of previous round).
**Round 3**     1ch, 14sc (work 2sc in every sixth stitch).
**Rounds 4–10** 1ch, 14sc

### LONG HORNS
Same as short horns until Round 3.
**Rounds 4–20** 1ch, 14sc

## EYES

Stitch eyes with two strands of red yarn.

## NOSE

Stitch nose with two strands of red yarn, forming a cross.

## EARS

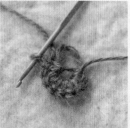   

1. Beginning with 10sc in a ring as before, increase every second stitch for four rows.
**Round 1** 10sc
**Round 2** 15sc
**Round 3** 22sc
**Round 4** 33sc

2. Fold ear in half and make 10 slip stitches to join the curved edge about halfway.

3. Attach the open end to head on an angle.

## FUR TRIM

1. Cut a 4 in. strip of cardboard and wind the white yarn around. Cut one end of the loops to make 8 in. lengths of yarn.

2. Insert the hook into the crocheted fabric, hook a piece of yarn halfway along its length and pull a loop through the fabric.

3. Wrap both tails of yarn over the hook and draw them through the loop. Pull tightly.

4. Trim the tails to length when all are complete.

## New beginning

The workshop is finished.
I hope the techniques you
have learnt inspire you to
make your own something
for someone.

thank you to you and

# felt me a smile

sunshine

kind

love

warm

happy

thank you to all animals and
haberdashery for inspiration

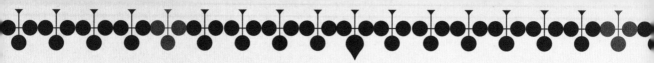

Published in the United States by Potter Craft, an imprint of the Crown Publishing
Group, a division of Random House, Inc., New York. Originally published in Great
Britain as *Pass Me a Smile: Heart-made Craft with Unconditional Giggles* by Murdoch
Books Australia, a division of Murdoch Books Pty Limited, Sydney, in 2009.

www.clarksonpotter.com
wwww.pottercraft.com

POTTER CRAFT and colophon is a registered trademark of Random House, Inc.


Library of Congress Cataloging-in-Publication Data is available upon request.

ISBN 978-0-307-58649-0

Printed in China

Design by Toyoko Sugiwaka
Step-by-step photography by Natasha Milne
Photograph of Winking cat tea-cozy (p. 103) by Mark Sariban
Figure illustrations by Carys Watterson

10 9 8 7 6 5 4 3 2 1

First American Edition

All the creatures in this book are smiling for you.

This is the story of the moment when I realized I am a bit
different from others. It was when I was a child, in Japan.
It was a sunny day, and I went with my family to a safari
park to watch animals.
The dolphins jumped into the sky with big splashes.
All the people there were laughing and shouting
with pleasure.
Tears sprang from my eyes without permission.
I couldn't clap or laugh at all.
Maybe I could hear the thoughts of the dolphins, "I don't
want to jump all day, I wish I could go back to the sea."

Maybe this is sentimental, but maybe it's true.

All the creatures in this book are smiling for you, even if
life is not quite what they want it to be.

Animals cannot explain their feelings in words, and they
just follow their heart.
If you follow your heart, like the animals, sometimes you
can find your nature, what is inside yourself. Every person
has an original way of thinking.
Use your instinct, and excavate the creativity that has
been buried.

When you are smiling,
when you are thinking of someone's
happiness,
the joyful wish is fulfilled.

Don't miss the wonder of small things –
they are all around you.

星に願いを  and the wish